HOW TO POO
AT WORK

This edition published in 2009 by Prion Books
an imprint of The Carlton Publishing Group
20 Mortimer Street
London W1T 3JW

ISBN 978-1-85375-740-2

A catalogue record of this book can be obtained from the British Library

Editorial Manager English language edition: Roland Hall
Design English language edition: Emily Clarke & Elle Ward
Production Controller English language edition: Claire Hayward

Page 12: Picture © Justin Horrocks/iStockphoto.com

Printed in Italy

9 10

HOW TO POO
AT WORK

MATS & ENZO

PRION

CONTENTS

Part 2: Problems on the Spot

Part 3: Problems on the Way Out

A crucial meeting *or* the man who ruined his career...

My first contact with the issue of how to use the toilets in a workplace goes back to the period when I was an intern in a big investment bank on Wall Street in New York. I was making databases on risk capital.

My boss was a very capable man. He had answers for everything and was a true professional. And yet, at 42, he was still on the lower rungs of the bank's hierarchy ladder. I couldn't understand it. At the time, I had not yet discovered the issues linked to the use of work toilets.

I worked quite closely with my boss during my internship and we became very close. Eventually, during our morning coffee, I gathered the courage to ask him why he had not yet managed to get a higher post in the bank. My question was met with a long silence. I could see in his eyes that he was annoyed by my question, but after about 30 seconds that felt like forever, he finally answered. He told me that one day, 11 years ago, he was hit with a bad case of gastroenteritis. Due to his infallible sense of responsibility, he decided to go to work anyway. At 10 a.m. he was overcome by horrific stomach pains. He went to the work toilet to try to get some relief from the pain, but as soon as he got into the stall, all of the members of the managing board of the bank, there for a management meeting, walked into the toilet where he was.

But the pain was simply too strong and despite the presence of all his bosses he had to relieve himself. The noise he made and the odour coming from the stall were proportional to the pain that he felt. Naturally, he wanted to get back to his office as soon as possible, but his bosses were still in the toilet when he emerged from his stall. He looked everyone in the eye and greeted them, apologized twice for the disturbance and tried to start a conversation by asking them how the meeting went. Only one of the bosses answered, by mumbling monosyllables.

Immediately he could see that he had just made a series of errors. In his panic he had broken all the Golden Rules of the use of toilets in a workplace.

I was stunned to hear that the use of toilets at work was governed by a series of rules which nobody had ever mentioned to me before.

He explained to me that from this miserable day onwards, he was nicknamed "stinkor" by everyone in his department and none of his bosses wanted him in their team despite the obvious quality of his work. I was sad for him but I knew that it was too late for him too. His career was finished; I could not help him.

On that day, I threw myself into the search for these Golden Rules and I decided that once I found all of them, I would share them with the whole world in a book, so that nobody else would ruin their career as my boss did. My success today is in part thanks to him. That is why I dedicate this book to him.

ENZO

The life of a company is a mix of written rules, public-spiritedness, hierarchy, good behaviour, often sympathy, sometimes hatred; of power but also influence, tasks and more. It is a tangle of complex rites that employees try to use as well as they can to achieve their personal goals within a company.

The codes of life in a company have become so complex that many magazines now exist that specialize in giving advice on how to survive, not to mention hundreds of books that deal with this as well. It is clear that it is now essential to read all this advice if we want to succeed in a company. We must educate ourselves to know how to be and how to do.

Many employees, executives, directors and so on invest much of their personal time in such reading. In their quest for perfection, these overachievers read everything that comes into their hands. Yet many of them will have wasted years and years of efforts to rise up among the best in mere seconds. The sad truth remains that none of these books give any advice whatsoever on the one place that many consider cursed: the toilets in the workplace.

What is the problem? None of the researchers, journalists, authors of books or philosophers have devoted their time to the question of the workplace toilets. Yet going to the toilet has been a real dilemma in the life of the modern employee. It is here that, confronted with the most primitive need, the hierarchy of the company is levelled; it's a place where the colleagues, bosses, secretaries and others all gain equal footing. Smells, noise, frequency of use, and toilets that don't work are all factors that can ruin a career. It is also highly likely that the first serious study to be made on this subject will find that hundreds of thousands of misadventures that happened in this seemingly innocent place have led to cancelled promotions, total loss of credibility for managing executives towards their secretaries, dramas that will not be forgotten and which can't be told to anyone. In your opinion, how many executives coming from big companies with separate bathrooms, for ladies and for gentlemen, lost their credibility when they moved to head up a smaller company and were faced with a unisex bathroom? How many others will abruptly finish their ascent to the top due to lack of education on this subject? And how many secretaries gave their bosses porcine nicknames just because they met in the toilet at a bad moment?

It takes only one time, one second, one misadventure, meeting once at a bad moment in the toilets of your workplace to ruin forever the image that you have built in the eyes of your colleagues and your superiors! I am also certain that all of you, without really thinking about it, have no doubt used some more or less effective strategies when going to the bathroom at work (going on a different floor, use of toilets at the other end of the hall...). This is because you know, deep inside you, that you have nothing to gain by going to the toilet, but everything to lose!

Fortunately you now have in your hands this book; the global reference on the subject. Already it has saved tens of thousands of careers on all continents and is about to save hundreds of thousands of others. Thanks to the advice that it gives, your destiny will never be shattered by a trip to your workplace toilets.

It interprets all the strategies to operate as adroitly as possible when going to the toilet, while you are in it and when you are leaving it. Finally, it unveils the tricks of the pros on the matter. Many techniques were inspired by the tactics of SAS experts, ninjas and Afghan tribesmen, but also included are contributions from anonymous inventive people who applied some pearls of creativity to prevent career suicides. After reading this book, you will know how to confront any terrain, avoid traps in any kind of infrastructure, even the oldest ones, and you will understand all the necessary techniques so that you will be able to confront even the trickiest situations with complete confidence.

And our goal? To permit you to master the techniques that guarantee safe visits to the toilet, without any danger to your career.

Enjoy reading... wherever you may be*!

MATS

* Some people actually read in their living rooms, and not just in bed like you do.

THE EXPERT: TOM HAYATT

Tom Hayatt has quickly become an indisputable authority on the subject of toilets in the workplace. It was he who first shed light on the issue in the prestigious *Management Journal of the Massachusetts Institute of Technology* in a 1987 article, "Real Social Working Dynamics for Water Closets". At first he was not taken seriously – due to the presumed lightness of the subject – but in 1992 he was finally recognized by his peers, especially because of the prestigious award given to him that same year: the Golden Toilet Brush. His name was also circulated for a while as a possible candidate for a Nobel Prize in economics. He is often associated with the acronym TML3S, a mnemonic tool used by many executives to keep in mind the dangers that lurk on the way to the toilets and to avoid any faux pas. TML3S stands for "Trace, Movement, Light, Shadow, Sound, Smell".

Tom Hayatt has circled the globe to speak at conferences. He is also regularly consulted on the proper positioning of the toilets in high-rise buildings.

THE GOLDEN RULES

The toilets at the workplace are governed by six clear rules. Even if they have never been written or formally defined, subconsciously everyone follows these rules. You can never break them, whatever the situation.

Rule 1: Never make eye contact with another person in the toilet

Rule 2: Never start a conversation with another person in the toilet

Rule 3: Create maximum distance between you and other persons present in the toilet

Rule 4: Never express what you feel inside

Rule 5: Stay impassive, no matter what may have happened in the toilet

Rule 6: Never make excuses in an effort to minimize attention to an event

Tom Hayatt has gathered these rules under the title "The Six N Rules":

1. No Eye Contact
2. No Talking
3. No Contact
4. No Emotion
5. Not Guilty
6. No Excuses

KEY TO SYMBOLS

Every problem is inspired by real events. For better visualization, the diagrams on the pages that follow represent possible situations.

These pages present all the depictions that are used in all the examples given in the book.

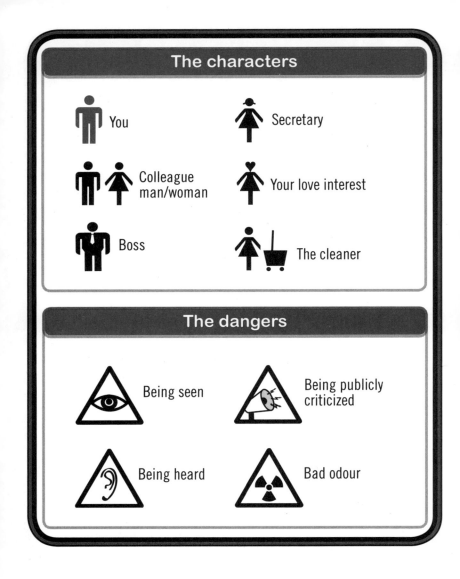

The characters

You

Secretary

Colleague man/woman

Your love interest

Boss

The cleaner

The dangers

Being seen

Being publicly criticized

Being heard

Bad odour

16

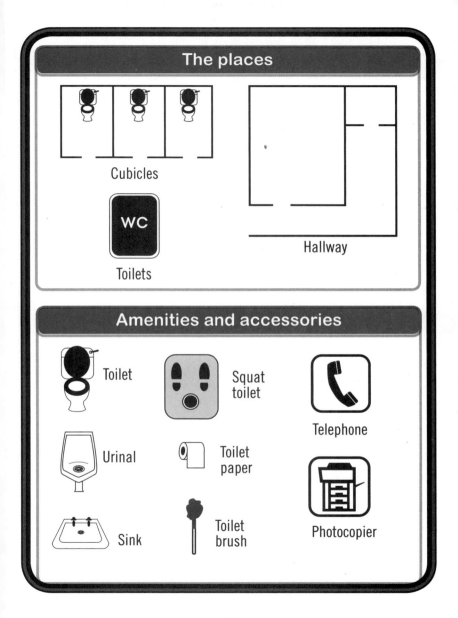

The places

Cubicles

WC

Toilets

Hallway

Amenities and accessories

Toilet

Squat toilet

Telephone

Urinal

Toilet paper

Sink

Toilet brush

Photocopier

17

Evaluation brushes

Each solution has been tested and evaluated in order to give you a maximum level of quality. Thanks to this evaluation you will have the necessary information before acting.

Each solution is evaluated on the basis of two principal criteria:
- realism
- difficulty level

For easy understanding, a "brush indicator" is used.

The higher the number of shaded. brushes, the greater the realism and the difficulty level.

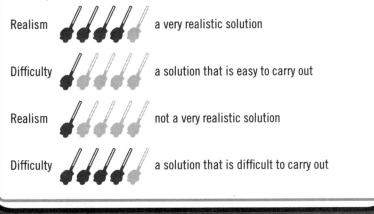

Realism   a very realistic solution

Difficulty   a solution that is easy to carry out

Realism   not a very realistic solution

Difficulty   a solution that is difficult to carry out

PART 1: PROBLEMS ON THE WAY THERE

The solutions to most typical problems that an employee encounters when going to the workplace toilet.

In this first part, we are going to tackle all the situations that you can encounter when you go to the toilet at work. We will suggest concrete and proven solutions.

PROBLEM: You are stuck in a meeting

You are in a meeting with your boss and your colleagues. You switched off your cell phone at the request of your boss, who does not want anything to disturb the meeting. Although you have been trying to resist for a long time, now it is absolutely imperative that you go to the toilet.

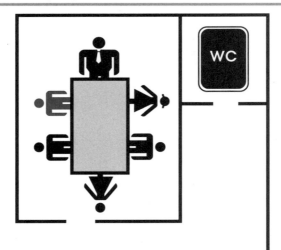

WC

Potential Dangers

SOLUTION: The method of four winds

1. Pick the quietest and most reserved colleague at the table (James).
2. Simulate loud flatulence while continuing to concentrate on the discussion.
3. Simulate flatulence again. Give your target a suspicious stare.
4. Simulate flatulence for the third time. Get up while exclaiming: "For heaven's sake, James, not done yet? We're in a meeting!"
5. Do not flinch at your boss's stare or your victim's protests.
6. Raise your voice and say: "Are you suggesting it was the boss?"
7. Sit down and simulate for one last time the sound of flatulence.
8. Storm out, yelling: "What a pig! I'll come back after you air the room."

Once you are done, re-enter haughtily, and: "OK, I'll come back, but James, restrain yourself this time. Can we now get back to work? Where were we?"

Expert Opinion

When I was working in a big company, I used to accuse the same colleague all the time. Though he never did anything, he was known as "fartman" to the whole company.

Testimonial

"I hate useless meetings on Fridays. Everybody is already in weekend mode and really not very focused. When I saw the guy next to me was half-asleep, I knew it was him I should accuse. Upon my return, the boss apologized and promised such a thing would never happen again. He actually admitted to the group while I was gone that it was him... How lucky!"
Tony, 29, software developer, Bristol

Realism:	Difficulty:

PROBLEM: You run into your boss in the hallway. He stops you and talks endlessly about his life

You are on your way to the toilet and you bump into your boss, who starts talking about his problems, his family, his dog...

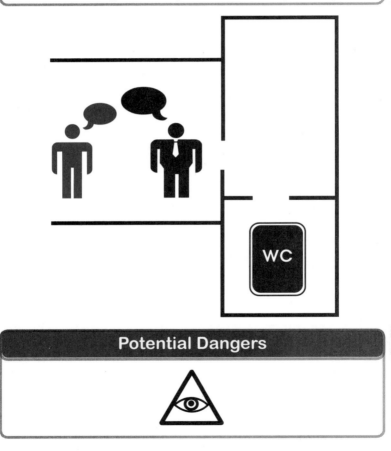

Potential Dangers

SOLUTION: The 30% method

1. Show no emotion (No Emotion). If you do, your boss might start asking you about your health and so on.
2. Pretend that what he is saying interests you. Nod and occasionally say: "Mm, yes of course, indeed, you are right."
3. Then change the subject to your work.
4. Brusquely ask for a 30% raise.

This will make your boss come up with an excuse, like an important meeting that he is already late for, and he will leave you alone.

Expert Opinion

This method is devilishly effective because it can be used over and over again. One can be sure that any boss will flee at mere mention of a raise. But before using this method, be sure that a raise is not actually very likely. If it is, your boss could invite you into his office, which will only prolong your wait and be very painful...

Testimonial

"In the past, all I could do was press myself to the wall, bite my lips and wait to be freed. One day, in a critical situation, I found the courage to use this method. I was even bold enough to ask for a 50% raise and the use of a company car. I can still see the expression on my boss' face; he immediately drew completely silent. Naturally, I didn't get the raise nor the car, but what I did get was a good laugh about it in the toilet..." Eric, 36, salesman, Hull

Realism: Difficulty:

PROBLEM: It is impossible to take a break

You are in your cubicle. The coffee break has already passed and lunch hour is still far away. You have to go to the toilet, but you are not allowed to take a break. Your boss is near, watching you.

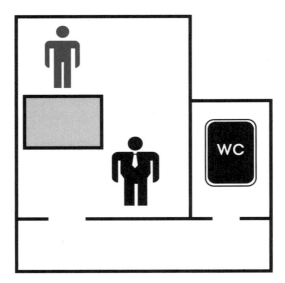

Potential Dangers

24

SOLUTION: Soccer tackle

1. Keep working silently, sitting on your chair.
2. Suddenly swerve to the side violently and fall off the chair.
3. Scream: "Aaaaaaaahhhhhhhhhhhhhh!".
4. Once you've fallen, roll on the ground, hold your head and pretend you are in awful pain (as a soccer player would do to get a penalty).
5. Keep showing you are in pain and make it clear that you have to see the nurse immediately.
6. Leave, alone, and do your business at the nurse's station.
7. Coming back to your cubicle, give a big, brave-boy grin to your boss and say: "You're lucky, I'm OK!"
8. Resume your work.

Expert Opinion

Careful, you could really hurt yourself. If that really happens, ask for time off. I think that suing your boss would be going a bit too far.

Testimonial

"I said that it was the guy next to me who pushed me. He got a company yellow card… I think I will get promoted before him."
Dick, 34, supply analyst, Colchester

Realism:	Difficulty:

PROBLEM: The cleaning lady is blocking the door

You have to go to the toilet, but a member of the maintenance service is blocking the entrance. You try to negotiate a way to enter, but in vain: the floor is still wet.

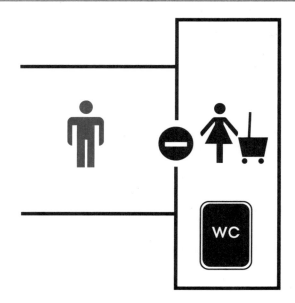

Potential Dangers

26

SOLUTION: The Java method

1. Stay polite and calm at the obstacle (No Emotion).
2. Go to the coffee machine and get a latte (a hot chocolate works just as well).
3. Upon taking the cup, pretend it is incredibly hot and spill it on the floor, feigning clumsiness (proclaim: "Oh no, I am *so* clumsy!")
4. Spill some on your clothes, so that you have an excuse to go into the toilet to clean yourself.

The cleaner will have to leave the toilet to clean up the mess you have made, and you will be able to enter, as you obviously have to clean up. Once you make it in, slip discreetly into a stall.

Expert Opinion

A method that works like a charm – but only one time! Of course, you don't need a double cappuccino dolce vita with extra cream; just take the cheapest coffee available…

Testimonial

"I will always remember the day, April 23, 2004. I was under a lot of stress on a work project, and had an overwhelming need to go at the end of the day. The Java method saved me. I lost a shirt, but I was able to save my dignity. Relieved, I was able to finish the project, and I was promoted."
Alex, 35, financial consolidator, London

Realism:	Difficulty:

PROBLEM: You are ill

You are at your desk, feeling sick and getting worse. Your digestive system is suffering, and you have to go to the toilet as a matter of urgency.

But the toilets are far, and the hallway is filled with your colleagues, chatting away. It will take some slaloming to make it to the toilet. When they see you running to the toilet, they will quickly know what's happening.

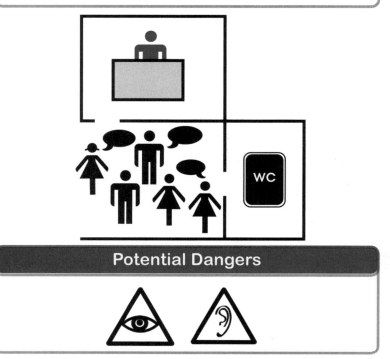

Potential Dangers

SOLUTION: Management giveaway

1. Reach for your phone.
2. Remember the name of the head of the HR department (Michael).
3. Scream: "WHAT?? Thanks for the great plan, Michael! Of course I'll tell them. Bye."
4. Announce proudly that the management is offering two weeks in Hawaii to the first ten who make it to the car park.
5. Count to ten. The path is now clear.
6. Run as fast as possible to the toilet, taking the shortcut in the building, which is now completely empty!

Expert Opinion

The method is tricky because you risk criticism from your colleagues upon their return. You could of course always defend yourself by saying that you too were the victim of a bad joke. In that moment, your dignity and your health are of course more important than being reminded of the situation every Christmas party. Incidentally, I am certain that some years from now, the security drill for evacuation of the toilets will be used as a model that will, in the future, serve as the fire drill.

Testimonial

"So my colleagues are stupid, and I had them with free cocktails being distributed by the HR guy at 10.30. The only consequence is that Albert, the HR guy, will never do me any favours anymore. But I would do it again if I had to."
Jeremy, 28, technician, Abingdon

Realism:	Difficulty:

PROBLEM: You are in your personal evaluation meeting

It is the end of the year, and you are in a personal evaluation meeting with your boss. You are in his office.

Potential Dangers

SOLUTION: A much deserved helping hand

1. Before your boss starts talking about you and your work, congratulate him on the work he has done over the year.
2. Tell him he must feel very tired at the end of this year that he spent working so tirelessly.
3. Tell him that you feel badly for him: he must not be thrilled to have to deal with even more paperwork right now.
4. As he starts to talk about what he calls the successes of the past year, take the evaluation sheet from his hands, and say: "Come on, let me help you!"
5. Mark "++" in all areas.
6. In the field marked "Suggested Salary Raise", write "current salary +£3,000". Sign the document by faking your boss' signature.
8. Leave the office quickly by saying: "You have always inspired me, boss."

Expert Opinion

Excuse me?! I have three employees and believe you me, it would never work out this way.

Testimonial

"I quickly filled out the evaluation sheet and I was perfectly reasonable with the suggested raise. Then I signed… but with my own name.
The intern in human resources thought she had mixed up names on the company personnel roster, so I got my raise and even a company car! My boss is disgusted: he had to give up his office…" Damien, 32, engineer, Norwich

Realism:	Difficulty:

PROBLEM: The toilet is next to the gossip queen's office

The office toilets are situated next to the office of the secretary, who is the company's gossip central.

You know that she will report to the whole unit any little detail on the noise and/or smell emanating from the toilet after you've been in it.

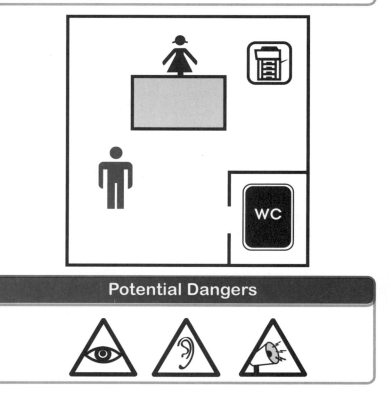

Potential Dangers

Solution: The scarf method

1. Go to the secretary's office. Tell her that the photocopier is broken and ask her nicely if she could go and have a look.
2. In her absence, take her scarf. Go to the toilet, and lock the door.
3. Use the scarf to insulate the door, so that no noise or smell can escape.
4. When you get out, go straight to the secretary's office, waving her scarf: "Look what I found in the hallway! I think it's yours, and I thought you would be happy to get it back, especially since it's so pretty."
5. Discreetly mention that perhaps the scarf has picked up some toilet odour.
6. When the secretary sees her scarf she will focus on it and won't even notice that you are coming from the toilet. In her happiness that you found her scarf, she will only be thankful.

Expert Opinion

How many bosses have had their careers ruined because of their vindictive secretaries, who gave all the details of their boss' performance in the toilet to the whole company? The efficacy of the method is questionable as it depends on the speed of your actions and the involvement of a scarf.

Testimonial

"Our secretary is very nice, but she has problems keeping secrets. Many of my colleagues have borne the brunt of it before. I therefore used the scarf method. It worked so well that I even got a chocolate bar as a thank you. Of course, I found her favourite scarf!" Ian, 45, grade school teacher, Kettering

Realism:	Difficulty:

You are on your way to the toilet. The moment you get to the toilet door, your boss appears and enters the toilet with you.

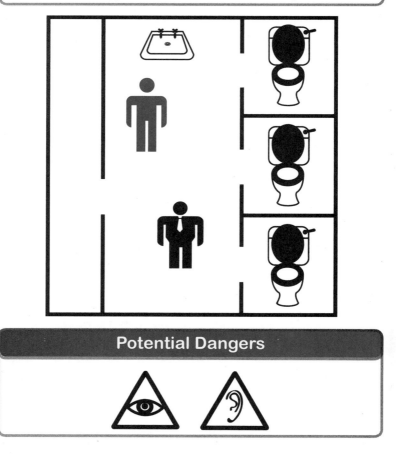

Potential Dangers

SOLUTION: Abort mission!

1. Keep your cool (No Talk); the situation is not as desperate as it seems. Don't forget that your boss also feels uncomfortable, because of your presence in the toilet.
2. Walk briskly and assuredly towards the basin. You want to make him think that you only came in to wash your hands.
3. Wash your hands and let water run to make as much noise as possible.
4. During the entire time you are in the toilet, the boss has to know, by hearing, exactly what you are doing.
5. Start the hand dryer.
6. Leave by closing the door loudly. That way your boss will hear that you have left and will feel free to do his business in peace.

Expert Opinion

It is highly likely that many of you haven't had to read this book to use this method, but as obvious as it may seem, this is the most effective method. Never risk ending your career by going to the toilet at the same time as your boss! What is more, imagine that he is one of those bosses who believes their superior position gives them the right to break the Golden Rules and, for example, starts to talk to you through the stall partition!

Testimonial

"I completely panicked when I saw my boss and couldn't exactly remember the method. I was so confused that I... washed *his* hands! I think it was the weirdest experience in both our lives." Joe, 37, property sales, Dubai

Realism:	Difficulty:
	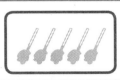

You are in your office, waiting for the person you are supposed to meet any minute now. Suddenly, you get an urge to go to the toilet.

Potential Dangers

SOLUTION: The long-distance call method

1. Call the person you are meeting with your number hidden.
2. Say: "Hello, this is your phone operator. We are verifying whether you made a call to Fiji yesterday that cost £1,492.65?"
3. Before he has a chance to answer, you say: "Wait, I will put you on hold for a few moments."
4. Go to the toilet and while you are doing your business, occasionally repeat: "Please hold, we are trying to connect you."
5. Once you are finished, say: "Thank you, everything is fine. You have, in fact, made a call for £1,492.65. Have a good day." Then hang up.

Expert Opinion

A classic! It is easy to carry out. Also, it gives you an added bonus: the person you are meeting will feel distracted after this experience and in a weakened position during the meeting.

Testimonial

"I had fun and made him wait for 25 minutes. I even made some background music by tapping my pencil on the bathroom door. When he finally showed up, I let him know that coming so late was completely inadmissible."
Peter, 32, sales manager, Falkirk

Realism: Difficulty:

PROBLEM: You are on a business trip in a foreign country

You are on a business trip to a subsidiary in another country and you have no idea what rules are in place in this country for the use of company toilets. Also, you don't know if "Toskityskitze" means "Gents". It could very well be that what you take for men's toilet is, in fact, the ladies' toilet, or even something completely different. The only safe way to do it is by making sure that you are alone in the room.

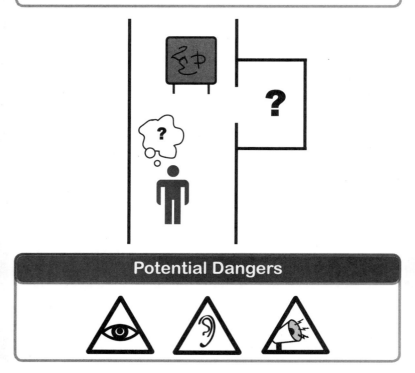

Potential Dangers

SOLUTION: The Trojan horse

1. As soon as you get to the building, locate the possible toilet.
2. Have a 6 x 2 x 2-foot cardboard box delivered to you.
3. Now, place the box in front of the supposed toilet and make two holes in it at eye level.
4. Get inside the box. Don't move, and make a note on your PDA all the comings and goings.
5. As soon as you are certain that the room is empty, enter the toilet and place the box in front so that nobody can see the door.
6. Do your business.
7. Leave as soon as possible.

Expert Opinion

At the beginning, I was often faced with this problem when I spoke at conferences in foreign lands. That is why I always came with a black briefcase, in which I carried a foldable box that I could put up when needed. Besides its obvious practicality, the black briefcase also gave me a more professional look, which contributed to my current stature. Today I am of course an expert in the rules that govern toilet use around the globe.

Testimonial

"My work often took me all over the world. This method has saved me several times. Once I entered a kitchen! Obviously 'Schterzai' didn't mean 'Gentle-men' as I had thought…" Michael, 37, export specialist, New Delhi

Realism:	Difficulty:

39

PROBLEM: You trick your boss, but he follows you

You are talking to your boss in the hallway and you come up with a strategy to make your way to the toilet without saying so. Problem: he decides to follow you.

Potential Dangers

SOLUTION: Health hazard

1. Speed up. He might stop following you at such a fast pace.
2. If he keeps up, tell him firmly: "Sir, with all due respect, you are slowing me down! I am young and do sports, and you are older; you used to smoke, and you are overweight. It would be much wiser for you not to follow me at my pace."
3. This could irritate him somewhat, but reassure him: "I hate to say such a thing, but I feel I must speak out, for your own sake and for the sake of the company, which obviously needs you very much."
4. Go to the toilet.

Expert Opinion

I would like to remind everyone that running too fast to the toilet stimulates the abdominals, which never helps.

Testimonial

"I tried to lose my boss, but he kept following me. After two minutes we were running down the corridor! And the worst part is that he actually beat me! He got first to the copy machine, but in the end that was OK because I could go to the toilet in peace." Leo, 28, account manager, Weymouth

Realism:	Difficulty:

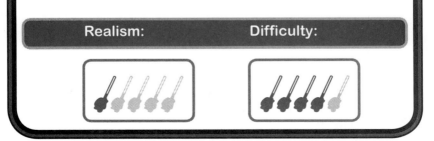

You are on the phone or in a teleconference and you have to go to the toilet urgently. This means that you must leave the conversation without anyone unnecessary noticing.

Potential Dangers

SOLUTION: The grenade method

1. Think of a question that people hate and nobody wants to answer. (There is at least one annoying task or subject in each company).
2. Interrupt whoever is talking by saying: "Wait a minute…"
3. Launch your grenade: "Tell me, Michael. Have you started on file X33E yet?"
4. Wait a few seconds while everyone starts shouting things like: "Oh, I thought Steve was working on it."
5. Leave the conversation by exclaiming: "I've had it, it's always the same! Fine, I am quitting this conversation and I'll call you back in 30 minutes. Use this time to come up with an answer!"
6. Go to the toilet.
7. When you call back, make it known that it was not a big deal after all and that you will talk about it some other time (nobody will protest).

Expert Opinion

A solution of great ease and one which works every time! And it has an added bonus: in your absence, others are doing the work for you…

Testimonial

"I was waiting for at least 30 minutes for the meeting to end so that I could go. Finally, I casually mentioned the case of Mrs Muffelton. When I returned to the meeting I was told that the case of Mrs Muffleton was resolved. This was great because it was really me who should have dealt with it."
Dominic, 22, client relations service, Sandringham

Realism:	Difficulty:

43

PROBLEM: You have to go for the sixth time in a day

You need to go to the toilet urgently, but it is the sixth time today. At this stage, you risk some prickly remarks.

Potential Dangers

44

SOLUTION: The big jump

1. Call Information.
2. Explain that you are urgently looking for a doctor specializing in gastric health.
3. Make an urgent appointment.
4. Once you arrive at the doctor's office, go to the toilet and relieve yourself in peace.
5. Then talk openly about your problems to the doctor. Remember, he is bound by doctor-patient confidentiality.
6. Take his advice seriously and treat your problem as he indicates.

Expert Opinion

If the doctor belongs to the company, use a colleague's name.

Testimonial

"*Again*? I had used all the methods there were to get to the toilet without my colleagues noticing, but I reached a point where I was out of ideas. I thought that it was time to see a doctor. Problem was that I asked our secretary to find me a number seeing as she is always talking about her father's health problems. But then the witch told everyone! How embarrassing... Now, every time I get up at work, my colleague chuckles: "Pains in the arse again?"
Terry, 39, client relations, Carmarthen

Realism:	Difficulty:

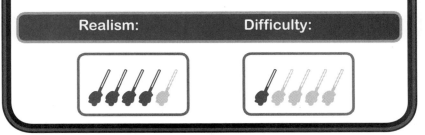

PART 2: PROBLEMS ON THE SPOT

Solutions for situations encountered in the toilets at your workplace

In this portion of the book we will tackle one by one all the problems that you might encounter in the toilets of your workplace. We will suggest the best concrete and tested solutions.

PROBLEM: The toilet smells when you enter

When you enter, the toilet reeks of a nauseating odour.
But it is too urgent, you have to use it anyway.

Potential Dangers

SOLUTION: The Rambo method

1. Don't vomit. (No Emotion).
2. If you are a man, remove your tie or your belt. If you are a woman, use a scarf, a belt or a shawl.
3. Take two pieces of toilet paper and make little nose corks.
4. Put one cork in each nostril and tie your belt or headband around your head in order to fix your nose corks in place. Don't tie too tightly as you risk making marks on your face.
5. Once you're done, take off your equipment and leave.

Expert Opinion

Remember to take out your nose corks before leaving the toilet. Companies often try to save a few dollars by not installing all the necessary toilet equipment. I once saw a computer company which reused their monitors as toilet seats...

Testimonial

"The architects who designed our building had a brilliant idea to put the toilet above the trash bins of our cafeteria. I can't even begin to tell you what Friday smells like..." Anne, 23, marketing, Glasgow

Realism:

Difficulty:

PROBLEM: There is only one toilet for fifty people

Your company does not follow the rules and has only one toilet for over 50 employees. People start queuing at 10 am; the situation is unbearable.

Potential Dangers

SOLUTION: The new high-tech system

1. Find a computer.
2. Write: "New procedure for use of the toilet: Due to continued abuse, a new system for toilet use is now in place. You will have one minute total to use the toilet. If you stay in longer than one minute, an alarm will sound, the toilet paper roll will fold into a storage box in the wall, the automatic cleaning system will come on and the door will open. We hope we will not have to go any further in our efforts to ensure order".
3. Install a little illuminated light box in the toilet, something to make people believe that the new system has really been put in place.
4. Distribute the notice among your colleagues and feign surprise and indignation at yet another brilliant idea from management.

Expert Opinion

If you can, try and get a revolving police light. It is very efficient, believe me!

Testimonial

"Since I put this technique in place, the toilet is always free. I am almost the only one who dares to go to the toilet any more. Better still, my bravery is admired by my colleagues!"
Frank, 25, product manager, Basingstoke

Realism: Difficulty:

After the deed is done, you realize that the flush doesn't work.

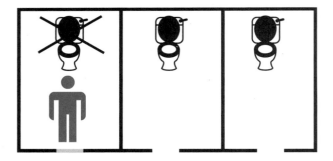

Potential Dangers

SOLUTION: The post-it of remorse

1. First, try three or four more times. You never know.
2. Take a post-it from your bag and write: "I am so sorry, I didn't know the flush was broken. I feel terrible." Sign it with a colleague's name (Paul).
3. Stick the post-it on the wall as visibly as possible. Close the toilet lid.
4. Leave the toilet head high (Not Guilty), as if you only just arrived. If someone is coming in, say: "No, use the other one! Paul broke that one."
5. Go to Paul's desk and reprimand him loudly: "This is the third time that you broke the toilet flush! You have to stop." Then add: "How old *are* you?"

Expert Opinion

Are there still people out there who do not check in advance that the flush operates? This is something so basic that we should not need to remind you of it any more. And if you get the bright idea to take up plumbing and fix the flush, I do not know where to begin to list the problems that could lead you to. Would you really like to risk drenching yourself at work?

Testimonial

"Before, when I was faced with such a problem, I would be completely distraught. At the time I used the only solution that came to my mind: I quietly closed the lid to hide my deed and tiptoed out in the hope that nobody would see me leave. But in such situations, as I'm sure you know, there is always someone waiting to use your toilet, so I always had to explain in embarrassment that I clogged up the toilet. Since I learned this method, I never fall into the trap and I don't have to change companies every six months." Ben, 37, manager, Brisbane

Realism:	Difficulty:

PROBLEM: The toilet is overflowing

You are in the toilet and you have just finished. When you flush, the water keeps rising and finally overflows.

Potential Dangers

SOLUTION: The Noah's Ark method

1. As soon as you see that the overflow is inevitable, close the lid.
2. Quickly climb on top of the toilet.
3. Grab the toilet brush and as much toilet paper as you can.
4. Throw the paper all over the floor. It will absorb the water. Then use the toilet brush to gather the wet paper in a pile.
5. Once the floor is dry enough, step off the toilet.
6. Without indicating that you were in the toilet (Not Guilty), call the cleaning service or maintenance and tell them there must have been an accident in the toilet...

Expert Opinion

What to do when nature unleashes its powers? How to avoid the shame and embarrassment when you have to face your colleagues with wet shoes upon your return from the toilet? Since cutting off the water would not help anything, this is the only method that seems realistic enough.

Testimonial

"I can still see myself jumping on the toilet seat to save my new suede shoes. I admit I was not proud of myself, but in this kind of scenario, you have only a fraction of a second to act." Annabelle, 31, PR, London

Realism:	Difficulty:

PROBLEM: The toilet seat is broken

You are in a toilet stall. After closing the door you notice that the seat is broken. You fear having an accident or getting yourself dirty.

Potential Dangers

SOLUTION: The spider method

1. Don't panic.
2. Tightly grip the coat hanger on the door to limit the pressure of your weight on the seat.
3. Make sure you keep your legs far apart enough to maintain your stability.
4. Even if you are tempted and it makes you go back to your childhood, do not make swinging movements as you risk making a noise or falling and making yourself look ridiculous.
5. Do what you came in to do.
6. Before leaving the stall, put the seat back into its normal position, so that people don't think you broke it. The next person will think s/he did it.

Expert Opinion

Practical and playful; I like it. Always make sure, however, that the coat hanger can take your weight.

Testimonial

"OK, I have to admit that I did swing on the hanger a bit at first, but when I had to concentrate, I stopped immediately. I'm tall enough, but I think a shorter person may have some problems." Quentin, 34, Exeter

Realism:	Difficulty:

PROBLEM: The person you like is in the queue

You go to the toilet. There is a queue in front of the door. The girl on whom you have a secret crush is in the queue. She must absolutely not know that occasionally you too happen to go to the toilet.

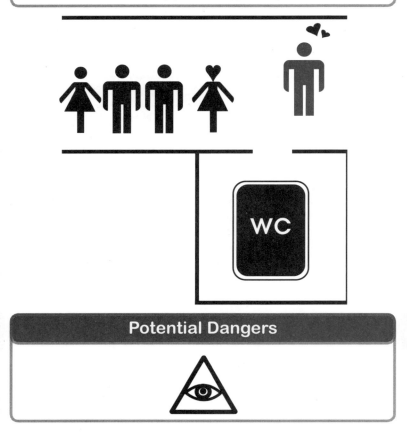

Potential Dangers

SOLUTION: Security

1. When you notice her, keep walking as confidently as possible towards the wall opposite the toilet door, so that you show that you were not in fact going to the toilet.
2. Go towards the fire extinguisher which is located in the hallway near the toilet door.
3. Take it off and remove the safety lock, all in quick and confident movements.
4. Start spraying (try not to cover people standing in line in carbon snow).
5. Say loudly: "It's all good, it works!" That way everyone will think that you only came there to test the fire extinguisher.

Expert Opinion

"This one time I will have to put on the laurels and take some credit. I invented this technique. You see, everybody knows that women have a soft spot for firemen. When she sees you confidently operating the fire extinguisher, she will immediately be attracted to you.

Testimonial

"I lost control of the extinguisher. It was a disaster. I prefer not to talk about it. And I am still single." Matthew, 34, engineer, Peterborough

Realism:	Difficulty:

PROBLEM: The toilet paper roll escapes from the stall

You are sitting on the toilet. The roll of toilet paper that you are using drops on the floor and rolls out of the stall.

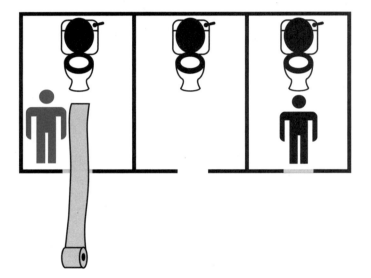

Potential Dangers

SOLUTION: Ariadne's Thread

1. Keep silent (No Talking).
2. Discreetly grab hold of the end of the roll that is still in your stall.
3. Slowly slide it under the wall into the stall next to yours, making it seem that it is coming out of there.
4. Leave your stall as if nothing happened.

Expert Opinion

Who has not tried to roll back the paper of a roll that rolled? The pitiful results of your work tend to make people lose their patience and throw the paper into the toilet. Every week, over 10 tons of toilet paper is wasted all over the world because of this! If your company follows the sustainable development policy, such behaviour is absolutely unacceptable. As for beginners, forget about the idiotic method of pulling the paper towards you, which only makes the paper roll farther and farther away.

Testimonial

"At home I make sure I don't waste paper. When it rolls off, I roll it back on. At work I have neither the time nor the patience. I don't pay for the paper anyway, so I prefer to put the blame on someone else. I now even get a kick out of seeing how far the roll went..." Marc, 42, head of services, Derby

Realism:

Difficulty:

PROBLEM: The booth does not close

You walk into a toilet stall and you notice that the door doesn't close. You can't leave.

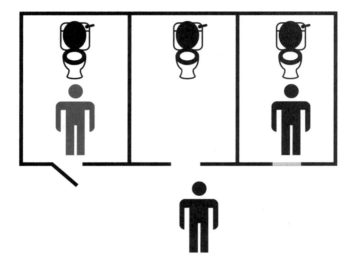

Potential Dangers

SOLUTION: The pound coin method

1. Find a pound coin in your pocket.
2. After you close the door, slip the coin under the joint, between the door and the frame.
3. If some space remains, put in another coin*.

*A pound coin is big enough to block the door so it doesn't open any more.

Expert Opinion

This is quite a sly method! I suggest you keep a pound coin or two always in your pocket when you head towards the toilet. I already knew the method of the toilet brush placed at an angle so that it prevents the outsiders from opening the door, but this one is even better. You would have to push terribly hard to bend a coin!

Testimonial

"Before I would always panic and look out for anyone that might pass. I was ready to throw myself at the door if anyone tried to open it and scream "Occupied!". Since I've learned this method, I am no longer worried when there is no lock. I always carry a pound coin in my pocket when I go to the toilet. I explained this method to a colleague of mine that I like. Problem is, he took a five-pound note instead, and even after folding it as much as possible, it didn't work..." Mick, 51, IT support, Liverpool

Realism:	Difficulty:

PROBLEM: Your boss must be in the next stall

Your boss wasn't in his office. You enter the toilet and you just know he is in one of the stalls.

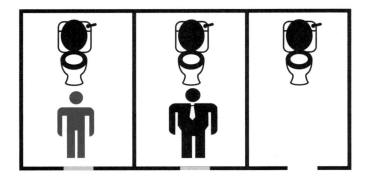

Potential Dangers

SOLUTION: Smoking out the beast

1. Just after you enter the toilet, turn off the light.
2. You should then hear: "Hey, the light!"
3. Turn on the light.
4. If you think you recognized the voice of your boss, turn the light off again to double-check.
5. With this, you should hear from the stall again, for example: "The light, damn it!"
6. If it is indeed your boss, leave the place immediately (turning on the light or not; depending on the level of affinity you have for him).
7. Come back to the toilet once he has left.

Expert Opinion

Never use the toilet at the same time as your boss. Do not even think about it! Do you want to risk jeopardizing your career? If you really cannot wait, step into the stall next to his and discreetly spray air freshener into his stall from underneath the separation. This will force him to leave his stall.

Testimonial

"Great tip! Before, when I wasn't sure if my boss was in the toilet or not, I would have to pretend that I only came in to wash my hands. This technique now saves me from making such pointless trips."
Caroline, 32, accountant, Tunbridge Wells

Realism:	Difficulty:

PROBLEM: Your shoes give you away

The stall door has a gap at the bottom that ordinarily facilitates access to the cleaning staff. It also makes your shoes visible and exposes you to the danger of being recognized by those who might walk into the toilet.

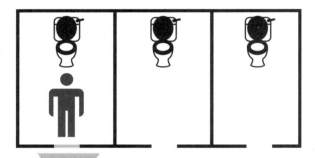

Potential Dangers

SOLUTION: Zen & opposing forces

1. Turn on your iPod.
2. Select soft New Age music.
3. Use the levitation method of the Tibetan monks from the Shigatse Monastery that you bought for £8,000 on the internet (beware: the £5,000 one sold by the Indian shaman is fake).
4. Levitate to about 4 feet (120cm). Be careful not to lift yourself too high, as people will then see your head stick out of the booth.
5. If you don't have £8,000 or if you have not yet mastered the techniques of the method you bought, try the opposing forces technique: push with your hands and legs on the opposite walls of the stall and try staying put as high as possible so that people won't see your feet.

Expert Opinion

It would seem to me that the opposing forces method is more realistic than the levitation method, but I must admit I have no competence in either domain.

Testimonial

"I've spent over £24,000 on the internet on different methods that were supposed to teach me how to levitate. It hasn't worked until now, but I think perhaps I am not training hard enough." George, 30, technician, Dawlish

Realism:	Difficulty:

PROBLEM: There is no toilet brush

You are getting ready to leave your stall. After you flush, you notice that there are visible traces in the toilet bowl. You would like to clean up, but there is no toilet brush.

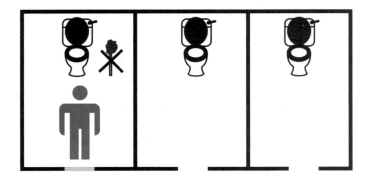

Potential Dangers

68

SOLUTION: The hidden present

1. Be very annoyed that there is no toilet brush.
2. If the circumstances are favourable (time, absence of others etc.), flush several more times.
3. If the problem persists, throw several pieces of toilet paper into the toilet and close the lid.

The next person will enter and close the door, lift the toilet cover and see the paper. He/she will flush before sitting down. This is when the person will find your hidden present... This doesn't solve your problem, but at least you are no longer the guilty one for those who will enter next!

Expert Opinion

Do not, under any circumstances, wrap your fingers in toilet paper to create your own brush. It NEVER works!

Testimonial

"Honestly, these absences of toilet brushes are becoming more and more common. In this day and age, with all the rising costs of living, I wouldn't be surprised if they're getting stolen by desperate employees. I did what I could with the flush. For the rest... as they say at the doctor's office: 'Next, please!'
Steve, 25, fork-lift operator, Braintree

Realism:	Difficulty:

PROBLEM: There is no paper in your stall

You are in a toilet with several stalls and you quickly realize that yours has no toilet paper. There is probably some in the next stall, but if you leave yours and go into another one, you'll look ridiculous.

Potential Dangers

SOLUTION: Extra stock

1. Find out if anyone is in the stall on the left by throwing some water over the wall. If an annoyed "Heeey!" comes from it, it means that someone is in this stall. Repeat the tactic for the stall on the right.
2. Slide your hand under the separation with the empty stall.
3. Feel along the wall with your hand and try catching the end of the toilet paper roll there.
4. Take a sufficient amount of toilet paper.
5. Finally, do what you came in to do.

Expert Opinion

Good method. If you can't catch the toilet paper next door with your hand, try climbing over the separation or sliding under it.

Testimonial

"I was just feeling out for the paper with my hand when somebody entered that stall. She saw my hand and ran out screaming. I think it might have reminded her of a horror film or something..." Piers, 43, publisher, London

Realism: Difficulty:

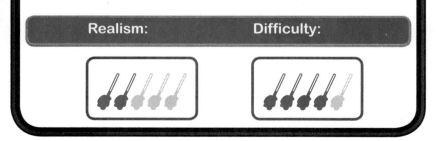

PROBLEM: There is no toilet seat

You go to the toilet and your toilet, which is particularly dirty, has no toilet seat. You would certainly not deign to clean it up yourself and cover it in toilet paper.

Potential Dangers

SOLUTION: The Golden Gate Bridge

1. Turn off the water.
2. Flush to drain the cistern. It will not refill because you turned the water off.
3. Remove the cistern cover.
4. Place it on the toilet so that it rests on both ends of the seat.
5. Take some toilet paper and clean any leftover dirt that might be lurking on the cover.
6. Sit on the cover, but be smart about it – think ahead about what you have to do to position yourself wisely.
7. Once finished, turn the water back on. The cistern will fill up.
8. Replace the cover and flush.

Expert Opinion

I must remind you here that companies who do not provide adequate sanitary equipment risk legal sanctions. A case came before the courts in the past that now represents a precedent: the head of a company tried to increase productivity by having all toilet seats removed (saving time and money). This man was found guilty of endangering the health of others.

Testimonial

"The toilets at my work are rarely clean. It never really works when I use the paper, and besides, it is not exactly hygienic or comfortable. I love using the cistern cover. I have to admit I even use it in service stations on the road, even if the toilet seats are fine. I don't want to gamble with my health!" James, 30, lab technician, Bodmin

Realism:	Difficulty:

You enter the only toilet available. The floor is very dirty.
It is winter and you are fully equipped (coat, suit, tie, scarf, laptop, and so on). As is often the case, your stall has no hanger.

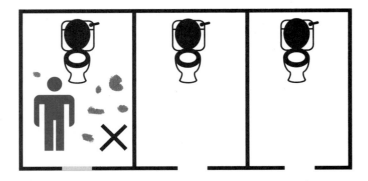

Potential Dangers

SOLUTION: The Ikea method

1. Don't panic. Toilets are full of hidden hanging equipment. You just have to be methodical.
2. Place your laptop vertically between the toilet seat and the cistern.
3. Take off your coat and place it on top of the water tank.
4. Remove your scarf and tie it around your head.
5. Take off your suit jacket and hang it on the door knob. After that, grab the door knob each time you hear someone enter the toilet. Anyone trying to open the door will make your jacket fall on the floor.
6. Unbuckle your belt and hold it at mid-calf level.
7. Stuff the ends of your trousers into your socks to prevent them from touching the ground. Flip your tie over your shoulder without loosening it.
8. Sit on the toilet and do what you came in to do.
9. Once finished, do all the steps above in reverse to be able to exit.

Expert Opinion

Be careful not to obscure your eyes with the scarf so that you can always grab the door knob when needed. Do not move too fast and do not mix up the stages of the process, like putting your scarf in the cistern.

Testimonial

"When I got into the toilet it was like a battlefield: water all over the floor, mud, paper sticking to the floor... But I couldn't help it, I had to stay. It took me five minutes to do everything and get settled, but I did it. I did panic a bit when someone tried to come in, though..." Carl, 37, consultant, Chester

Realism:	Difficulty:

You just finished and you pull on the paper roll, only to find just three measly leaves remain.

Potential Dangers

SOLUTION: The strips technique

1. Don't call out for someone to bring you more toilet paper. You are at work, not at home.
2. Pray to all the gods whose names you remember (even if only vaguely) that you have a packet of tissues in your pocket. Unfortunately, in this kind of situation, it is rarely the case.
3. Take the toilet paper distributor apart.
4. Pick up the empty toilet roll.
5. With your nails, cut off strips of carton, making them as thin as possible.
6. Use this as toilet paper.

Be careful not to make strips that are too thick or you may risk blocking the toilet.

Expert Opinion

Train at home to be prepared, should such a situation ever arise.

Testimonial

"I had to use this technique once in my life. It was horrible! I don't wish it upon anyone, and ever since I always make sure there is definitely toilet paper." Dominic, 43, car salesman, Newcastle

Realism:	Difficulty:

PROBLEM: Your colleagues arrive

You are the only one in the toilet. You have just sat down in your stall when a group of six of your colleagues enters the toilet.

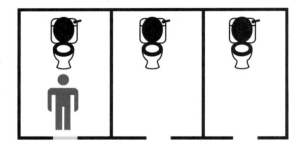

Potential Dangers

SOLUTION: Hall monitor, Mrs Lepasky

1. Get up and get dressed.
2. Leave your stall and look all your colleagues in the eye, one by one, saying loudly and strictly: "What's going on here?"
3. Keep your cool (Not guilty), even if your boss is there.
4. Pick a random victim in the group: "Well, Gerry, you think this is funny? Are you having fun doing your usual spiel, looking under the doors – and over them while you're at it?"
5. Then say: "Alright guys, that's enough, everybody out! Make a queue outside and enter one by one when I tell you!"
6. Once everyone is out, go back to your stall and do what you came in to do.
7. Go out and say: "OK, you can go in now, Jim."
8. Add: "Jim, keep your eye on Gerry. I can't stay here all day – I have work to do!"

Expert Opinion

A daring method, but devilishly effective. It will shock your colleagues because it breaks the "No Talking" rule.

Testimonial

"I stayed at the door and made them come in, one by one, in silence. They all obeyed. I was cracking up inside!" Laura, 35, mailroom manager, Stirling

Realism:	Difficulty:

PROBLEM: All toilets are taken

Your workplace is under-equipped in terms of sanitary facilities and more often than not your closest toilet is full. This means you have to go to a different floor or come back later, which can get very annoying.

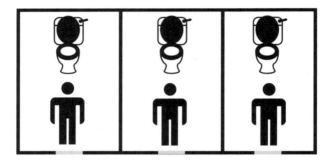

Potential Dangers

SOLUTION: Marking your territory

1. Wait until the end of the workday when everyone has left, then go to the toilet.
2. Close your eyes and think of the dirtiest toilet you can (in a nightclub, primary school after a water fight, service station...).
3. Reinvent the scene you just imagined in the toilet.
4. Splash water everywhere, unroll all the toilet paper rolls, write the dirtiest words you can think of on the walls (taking pleasure in this activity is completely acceptable).
5. Repeat the procedure every two days.

After a few weeks, the toilets will be considered always dirty by your colleagues, who, in turn, will apply the comparative advantages theory and start using toilets on other floors. The problem of the eternally occupied toilet will therefore move to the toilet on the floor below, and the one on your floor will become your personal toilet!

Expert Opinion

Don't go too far in marking your territory. Urinating on the floor is a canine behaviour, not human. Do I need to remind you of this?

Testimonial

"You have to be very organized and remember to go and make a mess in the toilet every couple of days. Personally, I noted it in my calendar and I partnered up with a colleague during the vacation period." Julian, 32, product manager, Winchester

Realism:	Difficulty:

PROBLEM: Your company installs eco toilets

In an effort to make a more earth-friendly company – the current trend for many companies – ecological toilets are installed in your workplace.

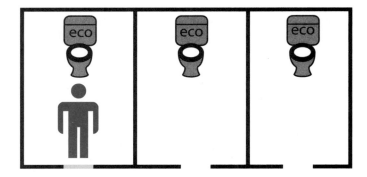

Potential Dangers

SOLUTION: Think eco

1. Don't panic.
2. Enter the toilet and draw the 100% cotton curtain.
3. Gently sit on the toilet, making sure you don't break the bamboo seat.
4. Do your business, but fight flatulence as much as possible (methane is a powerful greenhouse gas).
5. Use dry tree leaves in the same manner as ordinary toilet paper.
6. Once finished, pull the vine to make the rainwater run through the reed-bed and flush the toilet.
7. Rub the stone on the eucalyptus log next to the toilet to deodorize.

Expert Opinion

Who knows where this sustainable development craze will take us, twenty years from now? When will we use our bio-farts as an energy source to light up buildings?

Testimonial

"Imagine my shock when I saw that there was no door... Honestly, that took me some time to get used to. But now I have to say the concept has won me over and I will install it at home soon. However, the dry leaves are still a bit of a problem for me." Hal, 45, industrial designer, Manchester

Realism: Difficulty:

PROBLEM: Your phone keeps ringing

You are sitting on the toilet seat and your phone rings, revealing your presence.

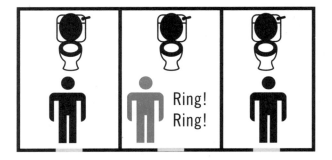

Potential Dangers

SOLUTION: The poisoned chalice

1. Find a website selling ringtones for mobile phones.
2. Pick a particularly annoying ringtone with the potential to really irritate your colleagues.
3. Give it to a good-mannered colleague of yours. (It is a gift, so he will feel obliged to start using it.)
4. Save it on your mobile phone as well.
5. After a few days everyone will know that the annoying ring comes from your colleague's phone.
6. Now make a habit of switching to this phone ring when you go to the toilet. If your phone rings while you are in the toilet, everyone will think it's actually your colleague who is in there. This means that from now on, anything goes: noise, smell etc. And it will always be your colleague who gets the blame!

Expert Opinion

Don't forget that even if you are dealing with a telephone, the "No Talk" rule still applies: you should never actually take a call while on the job.

Testimonial

"I gave Calvin Britney's 'Hit Me Baby One More Time' ringtone. It was the first gift anyone had ever given him since he joined the company in 1987. He had a tear in his eye. I've been using his ringtone in the toilet ever since…"
Alan, 33, logistics, Wolverhampton

Realism:	Difficulty:

PROBLEM: Your business phone falls into the toilet bowl

While unbuttoning, your work mobile slips out of your pocket and falls into the toilet.

Potential Dangers

SOLUTION: The dog method

1. Pick up your phone.
2. Leave the toilet.
3. Place your phone on the desk.
4. Use your office landline to call your work mobile phone.
5. Your mobile starts ringing. The vibrating shakes the phone and gets rid of the water (much like a dog that shakes to dry off – it's that simple).
6. Repeat several times, until your phone is completely dry.

Expert Opinion

I have my doubts about this method – it smells like an urban legend. Personally, I would never again place that receiver on my ear.

Testimonial

"I thought of this method when I was looking at my dog Fido drying himself off. Ever since, my husband calls my phone Fido and our dog Nokia."
Sandy, 53, receptionist, Merthyr Tydfil

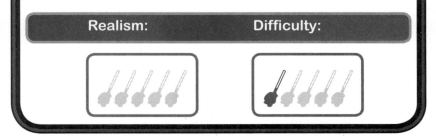

Realism: Difficulty:

In order to save money on maintenance, your company installs squat toilets. You are not familiar with the way to use such a structure.

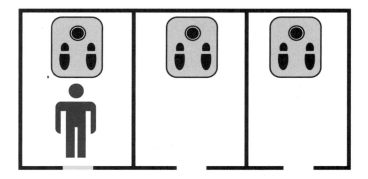

Potential Dangers

Solution: The tripod method

1. Pick up your laptop from your desk.
2. Walk with an expression of total concentration and in a quick pace down the hallway leading to the toilet. This will make your colleagues think you are busy and absorbed in a very important task for your company.
3. Once at the toilet, enter a stall.
4. Open your laptop at a wide enough angle, giving it a triangular shape.
5. Place it on the foot rests, with the sides of your laptop on the floor.
6. Use the laptop as a tripod to sit on it and do what you came in to do (don't forget to unplug your mouse).

Expert Opinion

Be careful not to drop your laptop into the toilet. Unfortunately, it is not equipped with the vibrating mode, making it impossible to dry it off as you would your mobile phone. Nevertheless, this is a rather efficient method.

Testimonial

"Since I've been using this method, everybody thinks I'm really busy and nobody in the company comes asking me to do something anymore. Triple bonus!" Pat, 31, paralegal, Slough

Realism: **Difficulty:**

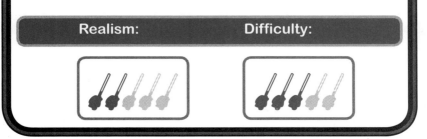

PROBLEM: Somebody knocks on the door

You are in a toilet stall with separating walls. Suddenly, you see the shadow of a person outside who is visibly in a hurry, pacing in front of your door. This person knocks on your door insistently, even though the door clearly marks that your stall is occupied.

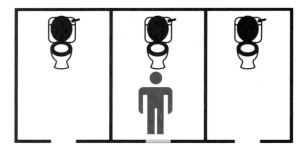

Knock knock

Potential Dangers

Solution: The mad toilet brush

1. Observe the shadow of the waiting person and their movements carefully. After a few moments of concentration you should be able to anticipate their next approach and knock.
2. Approach your door in silence.
3. Grab the toilet brush.
4. When the person outside is about to knock, slide your hand under the door.
5. In quick movements, swipe the toilet brush on the shoes and possibly also the trousers of the person outside.

The person outside will be shocked and annoyed, but will never knock on your door again.

Expert Opinion

Whatever happens, never leave the stall until you are done. Another possibility is to answer that person by knocking back on the door using Morse code.

Testimonial

"I admit I lost my cool at the fifth knock. I don't know what possessed me. I was trying to find a peaceful solution, but I lost control of my hand, which grabbed the toilet brush. I did not know I was capable of such an act! The funniest thing is that I found out the next day that it was my boss who was the victim of my toilet brush — he had new shoes on!"
Stephen, 33, magazine editor, Croydon

Realism:	Difficulty:

PROBLEM: Someone is waiting for you and you can't leave

You are ill and this makes it impossible for you to leave the toilet. Somehow, you are expected to attend a very important meeting.

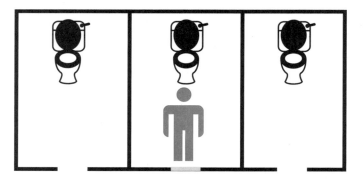

Potential Dangers

Solution: The technology method

1. Inform the people you are supposed to meet that you can't be there and suggest a videoconference instead.
2. Leave your stall and block the entrance into the toilet, as you will have to break several Golden Rules.
3. Return to your stall.
4. Sit down.
5. Turn on your webcam. Be careful: only your face should be visible.
6. Hook up your microphone. (Cough when you emit a suspicious sound that could give you away. For obvious reasons, do not use the technique of covering up your noises by flushing.)
7. Finish the meeting as quickly as possible.

Expert Opinion

My experience shows that the Golden Rules should never be broken, whatever the situation. I therefore do not approve of this method, which seems to me to be completely irresponsible.

Testimonial

"I'm embarrassed to admit that one day a while ago I had to do my video-conference from the toilet. It was the first time and I did as well as I could, but I made THE biggest error: I forgot to block the entrance into the toilet. Someone entered and surprised me. I panicked and the webcam fell into the toilet…" Kenneth, 32, Asia-Pacific accounts, Dover

Realism:

Difficulty:

You enter your company's toilet and see that a new, extremely sophisticated system has replaced the previous traditional system that you were used to. You embarrass yourself by asking a colleague — or worse, your boss — to explain how to flush the toilet.

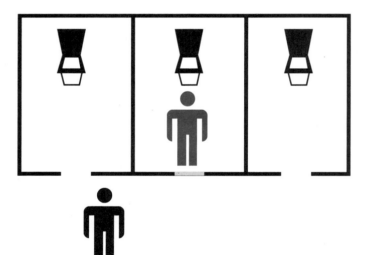

Potential Dangers

Solution: Extreme prudence

1. Do not hate the person who decided that the extra profits should be used on a new toilet system and not the raise which you have deserved for years.
2. Do not ask anyone for help, you have to figure it out on your own!
3. Approach the seat, remove the necessary pieces of clothing, but do not touch the seat. It may have sensors linked with the flushing mechanism.
4. Sit down, do what you came in to do as gently as possible and get dressed.
5. Once finished, do not flush: open the door of your stall first.
6. Close your eyes, cover up your face with your hands and quickly press on all the buttons simultaneously.
7. Run as fast as possible to leave the toilet and find a safe zone.
8. On the way, never turn back whatever happens, and never stop, whatever may take place behind you.
9. Take your hands from your face only when you have reached your safe zone.

Expert Opinion

When facing a new system, prudence is always a good policy. Usually such new systems are intuitive, but there are some importers on the market who do not translate the instructions from Japanese. Personally, I learned Japanese.

Testimonial

"When I realized that we had a new high-tech system in place, I thought to myself that this could be a new and interesting experience. Perfume spraying out, water rinse… Until I saw those tweezers coming out. I ran as fast as I could; I think I got out in the nick of time!" George, 33, assistant director, Stockton

Realism:	Difficulty:

PROBLEM: You create odours

You have just finished, and you leave an unpleasant odour behind. You leave the toilet and run into a colleague of yours, who is clearly on his way to the toilet.

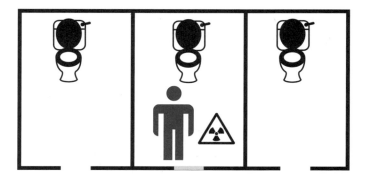

Potential Dangers

Solution: The blame game

1. Keep walking towards your colleague.
2. With an expression of shock, tell him that someone has left a horrible smell in the toilet.
3. Practise refusal or questioning to confirm that you are not the source of the smell. Say, for example: "I don't know who was in there but..." If possible, blame someone else who could be a plausible culprit. Say, for example: "I think it was Dennis, I saw him leave when I came in."

If the smell is unbearable, make sure you acknowledge that you too could not go in because of it.

Expert Opinion

This is a method that requires some cold-bloodedness. Accuse the same person as the one you blamed while you were stuck in a meeting 'Fartman'. If 'Fartman' is already well-known around the company, enjoy and have fun farting in the toilet!

Testimonial

"I felt horrible, the smell was dreadful. I'm shy by nature and I really worried about what my colleague might think, or even say, especially since he is known not to hold back his opinions. Just before leaving the toilet I thought of Michael from Accounts, who had just been bragging that morning about a boozy night out. I think that's what saved me..."
Maggie, 43, billing services, Weston-super-Mare.

Realism:	Difficulty:

PROBLEM: You make too much noise

You are seated on the toilet. A repeated 'splash', associated with the entry into water, risks alerting other people in the toilet to your presence — and what you are doing.

Potential Dangers

Solution: The landing cushion

1. Before sitting down, tear off a few pieces of toilet paper.
2. Throw them into the toilet bowl in a way that will provide efficient sound-proofing.
3. You can now attend to your business without worrying.

Expert Opinion

A very simple and widespread technique that is often invented on the spot by even the most uninitiated and basic user. Nevertheless, it seems to me, useful to present it in this book for those who haven't discovered it yet.

Testimonial

"Before, I would cover up the noise like everybody else: I flushed, I coughed, I tapped my foot, pretended I accidentally bumped the wall... I have now been using this new method. Through practice I have now developed the most efficient manner of placing the paper. But I am not telling. A good magician never reveals his tricks!" David, 43, lawyer, Lincoln

Realism:	Difficulty:

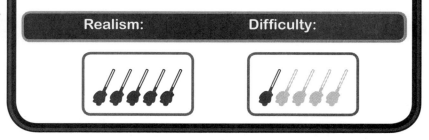

PROBLEM: You break the toilet seat

While using the toilet, the seat comes apart.

Potential Dangers

Solution: The delivery

1. Leave the toilet with the broken toilet seat in hand.
2. Look for a room with several people present.
3. Find a desk whose occupant is absent, then throw the toilet seat on it with force.
4. Take a piece of paper and write in capital letters: "When we break a toilet seat, we repair it! Thank you."
5. Before leaving, say loudly: "I'm sure he's gone off to break another one, the imbecile!"

Expert Opinion

Excellent example of the 'Not Guilty' rule application. A basic method one should always remember.

Testimonial

"The only empty office turned out to be that of my boss…"
Simon, 42, car park manager, Abingdon

Realism:	Difficulty:

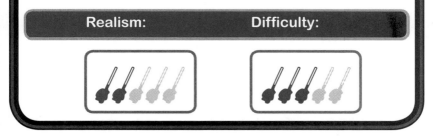

PART 3: PROBLEMS ON THE WAY OUT

Solutions to the most common problems that an employee can encounter while leaving the toilet.

In this third part we are going to tackle, one by one, all the problems that you could be faced with when leaving your workplace toilet. Once more, you will discover concrete solutions that have been tested and that are proven to work.

PROBLEM: You run into colleagues from your team who are coming back from lunch

You leave the toilet and, by sheer lack of luck, you run into your entire team and your boss. They saw you and therefore know that you just left the toilet.

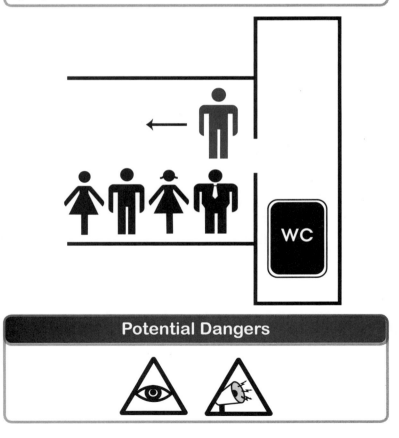

Potential Dangers

Solution: The weakest link

1. Do not show any sign of panic (No Emotion).
2. Identify as quickly as possible all the people in the group.
3. Pick the weakest one (Betty) and say: "Well then, Betty, there you are! I went looking for you in the toilet seeing as you are... well, in it all the time. You have to answer an email from a client; he's been waiting two days!"
4. Head back to your desk. While leaving, say loudly over your shoulder: "Sometimes I wonder how this place would run if I wasn't around..."

Expert Opinion

I would even suggest to Betty that she sets up her office in the toilet...

Testimonial

"I use a version of this solution. If my boss is not there, I always pretend I was looking for him. Yes, I'm a bastard, but isn't that how one rises in a company?" Tim, 28, assistant, Swindon

Realism:	Difficulty:

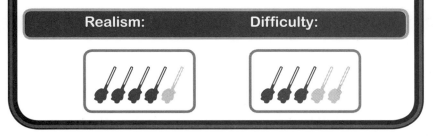

PROBLEM: Caught in the act: how do you re-establish your good name?

You have broken one or several Golden Rules and you did not use the TML3S (see Appendix, page 142). Several of your colleagues saw you and have been calling you unflattering names behind your back. You must re-establish your good name and reconstruct your image.

Potential Dangers

Solution: Image of purity

1. During the first year, do not go to any toilets in your company. Go elsewhere, the situation is extremely serious.
2. In the second year, go to the toilets at the same time as your colleagues and only wash your hands. This will allow you to slowly return to the toilets without all eyes turning towards you every time you enter.
3. During the five years that follow, enter the stall, wait three minutes without doing anything and then leave. You have to make everyone think that you are extremely clean.

If you follow this plan, you will gradually be able to repair your unflattering image, but you must not commit any errors during those seven years

Expert Opinion

Frankly, this solution is for utopians who live in a dream world. Because of the beginner's errors that you have committed, you are what we call a 'dead man walking' in your company. The faster you sign up at a job search website, the better it will be for you.

Testimonial

"I was wrongly accused of soiling the toilet on the third floor in a mass email. I even got 'pig' and 'Mr Yuck' post-its on my computer screen. I have been applying this method for three years now but without any results. I am at the end of my tether!" Jeremy, 27, technician, Milton Keynes

Realism:	Difficulty:

PROBLEM: You forgot to zip up and someone notices

You leave the toilet very discretely. When you arrive at your desk, one of your colleagues informs you that your zip is open. You are uncovered and have to repair the situation immediately.

Potential Dangers

Solution: The Arnie method

1. Don't show your embarrassment (No Emotion).
2. Take advantage of the fact that you have everyone's attention to show your power. To do that, stand up straight and puff out your chest.
3. Confirm that your zip was, in fact, not zipped.
4. Now say in a loud and confident voice these words exactly: "You know, in humans, 89% of testicular cancer cases are due to insufficient ventilation. The remaining 11% comes from physical harm. So start working instead of looking at my zip, or I'll add you to the 11% statistic!"
5. If you have managed to keep your colleague's breathless attention, add gracefully: "Actually, your wife is cheating on you... for about five years now."

Expert Opinion

When faced with remarks regarding your zip it is of capital importance that you immediately re-establish order, while keeping the Golden Rules in mind. This method, although somewhat brutal, helps you reach this objective.

Testimonial

"I am a bit of a scatterbrain and I forget to zip up my trousers a few times in the past to. Although one little remark can be amusing, constant repetition can get a bit annoying. When I changed jobs I decided to apply the Arnie solution. And it worked! My colleagues now walk around with flies open, and I get bought coffee without even asking for it!"
Sam, 32, call center employee, Southend

Realism: Difficulty:

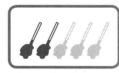

109

PROBLEM: The Men's was closed and you went to the Ladies'

The men's toilet was shut, and you had to use the women's. When leaving, a female colleague shoots you a reproachful look.

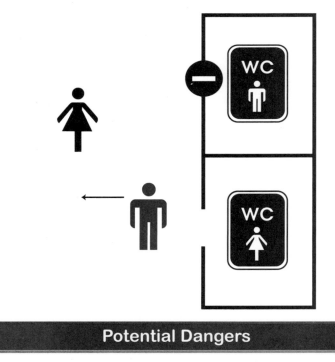

Potential Dangers

Solution: Under-the-belt feminist

1. Leave the toilet with confidence (Not Guilty).
2. Hold the look of your colleague.
3. Tell her in a firm tone: "You want equality with men in the company – now you have it! From now on, we use your toilet. We'll do what we have to do!"

Expert Opinion

A bit too risky for my taste! And I am not in favour of male/female equality. If we are not equipped in the same way to go to the toilet, we are not equal in the use of the facilities. End of negotiation!

Testimonial

"I had no other option but to go to the ladies' room, and then stick to the approach proposed in this solution. My male colleagues think of me as a hero, but my female colleagues have taken to calling me Francine! The war is on!"
Frank, 34, major account manager, Chichester

Realism:	Difficulty:

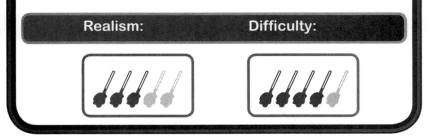

PROBLEM: You leave traces of your trip behind

You leave the toilet, but you have made the stall, as well as the floor in it, dirty. The toilet was clean before you entered.

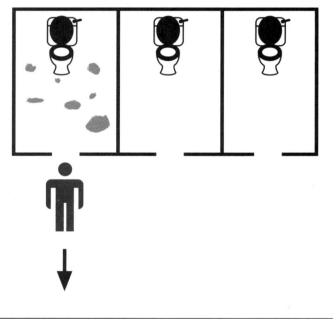

Potential Dangers

Solution: In bad faith

1. Take a felt-tip pen.
2. Above the sign that says: 'Keep this place as clean as you found it', write: "I found this place dirty, I left it dirty – did I do the right thing?"
3. Return immediately to your desk.
4. Send an email to the whole company. Subject: "Toilet vandalism".
5. In the body, write this: "One of you has dirtied the toilet and amused himself by writing a line of dubious humour on the sign. In the name of the whole company, I would like to ask this person to stop immediately this childish behaviour and start behaving like an adult in the toilet. P.S. George, we all think it was you. Admit it and I think many among us will forgive you."

Expert Opinion

Interesting solution. I have always found such signs stupid.

Testimonial

"Everybody was sure that the colleague I mentioned in the email was the one who did it. He really had it in for me since then. I apologized to him and told him that while maybe I was wrong, I did this in good faith."
Andy, 42, financial analyst, Scarborough

Realism:	Difficulty:

PROBLEM: The lock is broken, you can't unlock the door

You are in a stall and the door lock becomes blocked. The bathroom stalls are equipped with dividers, with openings above and below.

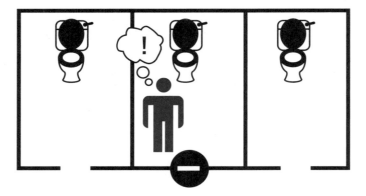

Potential Dangers

Solution: The fax method

1. Stay calm and try one more time to open the door normally. Quietly take off all pieces of clothing limiting your movement. Place them under the door.
2. Climb onto the toilet, then measure the distance between separator and ceiling. Compare it to your waist. If there is enough space, continue.
3. Stand on the toilet, hands on top of the dividers each side.
4. Swing your left leg over the top of the door. Repeat with your right leg.
5. Like a fax, slide out. Watch out for any lights that might be on the ceiling.
6. Jump down on the other side of the door.
7. Leave tranquilly. If you were seen, whistle jauntily whilst walking away.

Expert Opinion

Every year we witness dozens of serious accidents that happen to people who have not measured the space between the door and the ceiling, and who get blocked in the company toilets for a whole weekend. The designers are now obliged to leave a space large enough to allow for the passage of all body types (also known as a safety passage).

Testimonial

"I once got stuck in a toilet stall with a blocked lock. In panic, I called for help. My colleagues came and helped me get out by making a human ladder outside the door. I got out, but I had to suffer the embarrassment of it for years. Everybody in the office now calls me Mr. Sticky. I would now never hesitate to try to climb out on my own, even if it you risk a cracked rib!"
Peter, 24, journalist, Belfast

Realism:	Difficulty:

PROBLEM: You splash water all over yourself while washing your hands

You leave the toilet and wash your hands, but you splash water on your trousers by accident. The stains could be deemed suspicious and give the impression that this is not necessarily water.

Potential Dangers

Solution: The leopard's fur method

1. Examine the affected area carefully.
2. Wet your hands.
3. Using small wrist movements, splash water gently on your shirt (on the sleeves and above your waist).
4. Leave the toilet looking annoyed.

If a colleague looks at you, complain to him: "I'm sick and tired of these old sinks we have – the water goes all over the place!"

Expert Opinion

In my line of work I visit thousands of toilets every year. I regularly face men who are trying to dry their pants with an electric drier. You should see their faces when they realize someone is watching them!

Testimonial

"One day I got water on my trousers just before a meeting. With my usual luck, it looked really suspicious… But this time, instead of trying to wipe it off, I splashed some water above the waist to mask the accident. When I got to the meeting, my boss told me that this has happened to him too. Fine, but everyone knows that he never washes his hands… What a pig!"
Daniel, 36, legal expert, Penzance

Realism:	Difficulty:

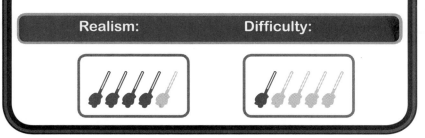

PROBLEM: You find yourself in front of the person you are in love with

When leaving the toilet, you find yourself in front of a person with whom you are desperately in love and who works in another department.

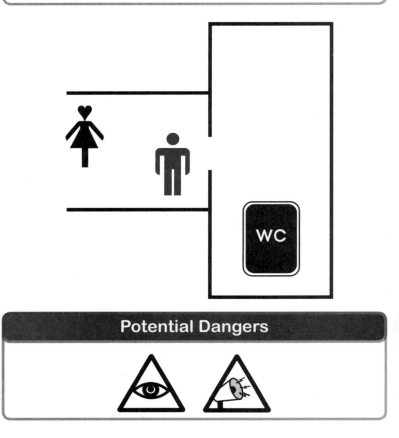

Potential Dangers

Solution: The secret agent method

1. Leave the toilet (Not Guilty).
2. Close the door delicately.
3. Throw your jacket over your shoulder with a cool elegance.
4. Now, straighten your torso and gaze into the distance with your look of a dominant male.
5. Walk towards your office confidently and elegantly.

Expert Opinion

I am an expert in Real Social Dynamics for Toilets at Work, and not a Love Coach. I hate it when people who know nothing about my field give their opinions on it. I will therefore not comment on this solution in my expert capacity. However, if you want my personal opinion: you never had the courage to talk to this person, so she probably doesn't know who you are, what you do, or even that you work in the same company as she does. In a maximum of one minute, she will have forgotten ever seeing you. Moreover, you have probably completely idealized her, when in reality she is probably stupid and has nothing to talk about. You would do better to concentrate on your attitude in the toilets towards your colleagues and your boss! Don't forget, it is your career that is on the line.

Testimonial

"For two years I played cool when leaving the toilets and saw Elisabeth nearby. One day I had to go see her to ask for a document. She didn't recognize me and even wanted to see my badge to make sure I worked in the same company. I was crushed." Anthony, 36, planner, Toronto

Realism:	Difficulty:

PROBLEM: It is impossible to wash your hands and you are seen leaving

You leave the stall and you can't wash your hands.
Then you leave and a colleague sees you.

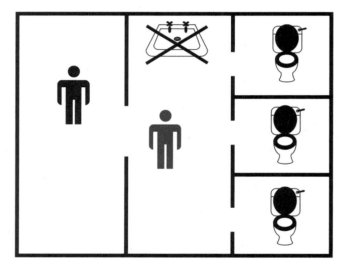

Potential Dangers

Solution: The moonwalk method

1. Keep silent and stay unbothered (No Talking, No Emotion).
2. Make a quick half-turn.
3. Do a Michael Jackson moonwalk back towards your office.

Your colleague will be completely absorbed by this curious manner of walking, giving the impression that you are walking forward while really you are moving backwards! Hypnotized by your walk, he will completely forget that you haven't washed your hands.

Expert Opinion

Of course you cannot moonwalk on carpeted floor. I suggest taking off your shoes to facilitate this.

Testimonial

"My father is a Michael Jackson fan, so I knew the moonwalk and that helped. To be even more efficient, I added arm movements to it, street dance style. I told a colleague about this method, but he has two left feet when it comes to dancing. However, he was a gymnast in the past so he had an idea. He returns to his office by doing a series of backflips, summersaults and piked landings." Michael, 22, courier, Luton

Realism:

Difficulty:

PROBLEM: You come across your boss

You leave the toilet and you bump into your immediate boss who is heading there himself.

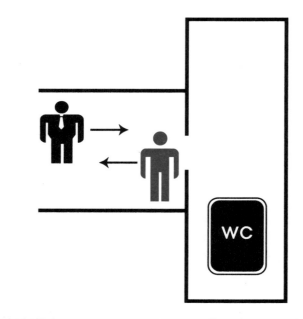

Potential Dangers

Solution: The mirror method

1. Don't talk (No Talking).
2. Keep looking down; your boss will do the same thing.
3. Move towards the wall until you are almost touching it (No Contact). Your boss will move towards the wall on his side. Be careful not to knock off the fire extinguishers.
4. When you are finally next to each other, stay calm and do not show any sign of weakness (No Emotion, Not Guilty, No Excuses).
5. Once your boss is in the toilet, start behaving normally.

Expert Opinion

In this kind of situation, only the Golden Rules can save you. This method is perfect – apply it meticulously.

Testimonial

"I don't know why, but I have a gift for running into my boss all the time! Now I know what to do. We found our balance in this way. We stick to it so precisely that there are even marks on the carpet where we pass!"
Henry, 43, technician, Wrexham

Realism:	Difficulty:

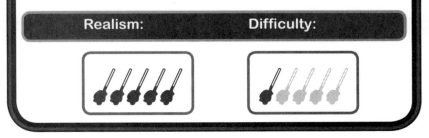

PROBLEM: One of your colleagues stinks it up next door and you have to leave

There are several people in the toilet at the same time as you. A colleague of yours is in the stall next to yours. He makes noise and a horrendous smell is coming out of his stall. Someone could think that it is emanating from yours.

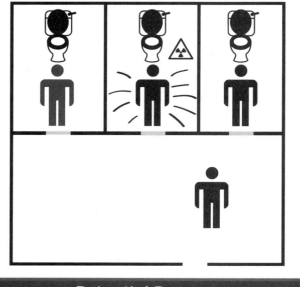

Potential Dangers

Solution: The rescue method

1. Finish doing what you came to do as quickly as possible.
2. Precipitously leave your stall.
3. Open your neighbour's door with force, using either your shoulders or legs.
4. Grab your colleague and push him out of the stall.
5. Lay him on the floor and start CPR (cardiopulmonary resuscitation).
6. He will say: "Stop it! Are you crazy?"
7. At this, you say: "Oh my God, you are alive! You know, with the noise and the smell that you were making, I thought your digestive system had exploded!" Now everyone present will know that it wasn't you who was responsible for the awful noise and smell.
8. Leave like a hero.

Expert Opinion

You will become known as someone who is ready to do anything to save a colleague. Excellent!

Testimonial

"When I knocked down the door, it hit my colleague. I had to do the resucitation for real!" Paul, 57, accounting manager, Inverness

Realism:	Difficulty:

PROBLEM: Your shirt gets stuck in your zip

You are getting ready to leave your stall. While getting dressed, your shirt gets stuck in your zip. A piece of fabric is now sticking out of your zip. You try to gently pull it out, but it is impossible. If you go back into the office with a piece of fabric coming out of your zipper, you risk the mean remarks of your less-than-delicate colleagues.

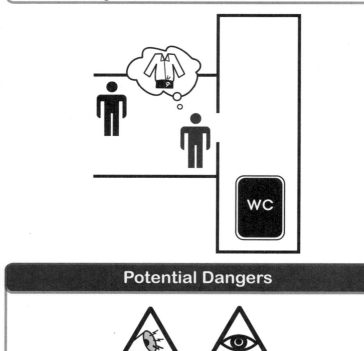

Potential Dangers

Solution: The Hulk method

1. Forget the price you paid for the shirt and trousers (clearly, your image in the company is worth much more).
2. Persuade yourself that you can't leave in this way and risk being ridiculed.
3. Grab your trousers firmly and swiftly, and violently pull your shirt out. It will tear, and your zip will break.
4. Tuck your shirt into your trousers and close the button of the trousers.
5. When you leave the toilet, walk towards your office with your arms up. This will create diversion: your colleagues will concentrate on your arms and will not notice that your zip is open.
6. After that, stay seated behind your desk, whatever may happen.
7. Be the last to leave the office, using poorly-lit corridors.

Expert Opinion

Don't hold back in arm movements while walking down the corridor. Whatever your colleagues' attitude may be, respect scrupulously the No Eye Contact, Not Guilty, No Emotion and No Talking rules.

Testimonial

"Of course this happened to me at 8.30 in the morning on the day that I wore my favourite suit and shirt. I could not leave before 23.40, and I can tell you, that was a long day. I now use my shirt to clean the windows of my studio apartment. My grandmother managed to repair my trousers, but this doesn't really console me..." Liam, 38, consultant, Canterbury

Realism:	Difficulty:

Before you left the toilet, you generously sprayed it with air freshener. The problem is that now you too smell of "pine tree with lavender" and you have to return to your office.

Potential Dangers

Solution: "Whoever smelt it, dealt it"

1. Even though you are carrying a very particular smell, walk normally.
2. Sit down at your desk.
3. After a few seconds, someone will ask: "Is it me or... do you smell pine?"
4. Do not show any sign of hurt feelings.
5. Take a deep breath (but remember, you stink of pine with lavender).
6. Say: "Yes. Your B.O. is so vile I had to put on air freshener to mask it!"
7. Add: "You should sort it out. I'm not the only one who thinks so."
8. Go back to your work.

Expert Opinion

Body odour in a workplace, now that's a prickly subject! I have always wondered what is more unpleasant in the toilet: the smell left by its previous user, or the smell of air freshener. It is certainly the mix of the two! That is why I have been an active member for several years now of an association that fights against the use of air fresheners in toilets. It is because I prefer a 'natural' smell rather than 'natural' mixed with flowers!

Testimonial

"The first time this happened to me I went out to buy some flowers before returning to my desk. I said it was to liven up the place a bit. I even put on a Hawaiian flower necklace. The second time I accused my colleague. He asked to change teams. I think I may have gone too far."
Jeff, 37, geological surveyor, Redbridge

Realism:	Difficulty:

MEN-ONLY PROBLEM:
How to use urinals

Our expert Tom Hayatt has informed us that he receives a lot questions about urinals. Upon his advice, and despite the fact that the subject is not entirely on the same level as the rest of this book, we have decided to dedicate a feature to it.

Example 1:   Example 2:

Example 3:   Example 4:

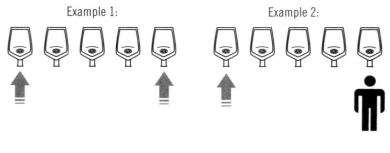

Expert Explanation

1. Urinals are found within the sanitary facilities. As a consequence, their use is governed by the same rules.
2. You can never look into the eyes of the person who is using the urinals at the same time.
3. Similarly, you must not start a conversation with another user (in any case, he will not respond).
4. You must not express your feelings (such as sighing an "mmmmmm" in relief).
5. Stay calm and composed whatever may happen.
6. Do not excuse yourself if you commit an error (flatulence, bad aim…).
7. Always maximize the difference with other users.
8. In short, simply apply the Golden Rules.

Let us spend a little more time on one of the key rules for use of urinals and look at how to best apply the Distance Maximization rule.

Example 1: all urinals are available
You must use the urinal at either end of the urinal wall. This can be either on the left or right, it's not important. That way, if someone comes in, he can use the urinal at the other end.

Example 2: someone is already using a urinal
You have to use the urinal that is at the greatest distance from his.

Example 3: two other users are present
You have to maximize the distance that separates you from two other users.

Example 4: three other users are present
In this situation you cannot use the urinals. A courtesy urinal should always separate the users.

Attention: On no account use the urinal that is smaller than others, shaped slightly differently, and protected by a bar or equipped with a flush that is a bit curious. This is not a urinal: it is an installation used for the storage of cleaning products.

MEN-ONLY PROBLEM:
Only urinals

You get to the toilet, but there are only urinals.

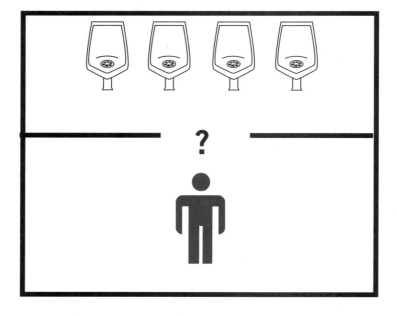

Solution: The Niagara Falls

1. Stay calm in the face of the challenge. (No Talking, No Emotion). Don't panic; tell yourself that you are not the first to encounter this problem.
2. Keep your back straight, suck in your belly and think of Niagara Falls.
3. Visualize the Falls and listen to the falling water.
4. Now, take ten deep breaths and tell yourself that you only have to urinate anyway.

Urinate and leave as quickly as possible.

Expert Opinion

Do not even try to relieve yourself in a urinal in any other way than that for which it was intended. Trust me!

Testimonial

"I have to admit I cursed for a while that day! I do not understand how it is possible in the twenty-first century to still have such installations in a company! When leaving the toilet I met someone who runs a yoga club. I signed up and at the end of this year we are leaving on a trip to… Niagara Falls! I guess something good can come out of anything!"
Terry, 40, warehouse manager, York

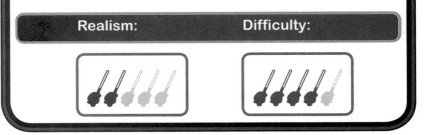

Realism: Difficulty:

WOMEN-ONLY PROBLEM:
Handbag etiquette

You went to the toilet discretely, but you left your handbag behind. One of your colleagues brings the bag to you in the office.

Potential Dangers

SOLUTION: The killer boomerang

1. Do not say thank you. Pretend to be surprised.
2. Say: "Sorry, but this is not mine. You must be mistaken."
3. If your colleague insists, keep denying.
4. Take advantage of the situation to improve your image in the company and say loudly and clearly that you do not use the toilet at work.
5. Seeing as your colleague is your direct competitor in the company, go further. Ask her loudly: "Anyway, what were you doing in the toilet?"
6. Worried and weakened, she will answer: "Ehmm, I went to wash my hands."
7. Answer: "Oh yeah? It takes you 20 minutes to wash your hands? And this bag stinks... Honestly, I think everyone here has understood what you were doing in the toilet."
8. Tell her to leave the bag at the reception, where its owner will surely come looking for it.
9. At the end of the day, carefully pick up your bag from reception.

Expert Opinion

Go even further and say that this is a conspiracy against you and your career.

Testimonial

"In panic, I accused my colleague of having stolen my bag. Not only did nobody believe me, but everyone now knew that I went to the toilet. It happened 11 years ago, and I still hold the same position; I have never been promoted." Olivia, 41, marketing manager, Letchworth

Realism:	Difficulty:

WOMEN-ONLY PROBLEM:
A colleague follows you

You made friends with a colleague, and now she always goes to the toilet with you. Given what you have to do this time, you would prefer to go alone. But the moment you head to the toilet, she is up and following you.

Potential Dangers

SOLUTION: The limit

1. Don't look embarrassed.
2. As if nothing is wrong, go together to the toilet as you have been doing lately.
3. On the way, pretend to get uncomfortable and say: "Listen, I shouldn't be telling you this, but the boss has noticed that you go often to the toilet."
4. When she acts incredulous, continue: "Yeah, he has an Excel file where he marks comings and goings... Apparently you're at the top of the list and about to reach the limit..."
5. This should make your colleague turn around immediately and return to her desk, worried and appalled at the same time.
6. When you return, go to her and start gossiping about your boss like you always do.

Expert Opinion

I still do not understand why women go to the toilet together. They even talk in there! What about the Golden Rules?

Testimonial

"In my previous job I had a colleague who was nice, but a bit clingy. To make her stop following me to the toilet, I came up with a story that the financial director had told me he often came to the ladies' toilet and aimed at the toilet seats. I added that our IT guy had placed hidden webcams and that the cleaning was only done every six months. But this method backfired, since then she thought that I was a disgusting exhibitionist who used the toilet despite all that..." Christina, 34, accountant, Wisbech

Realism:	Difficulty:

You said you had to go and powder your nose, but a male colleague with a distinct lack of class tells you that your make-up looks just as it did before.

Potential Dangers

Solution: The femme fatale

1. Don't say what you were really doing. Many men still believe that women actually go to powder their noses.
2. Respecting the "No Emotion" rule, pretend to be surprised and say: "Aw shucks, looks like my make-up really isn't holding on today."
3. Since your colleague thought he was being crafty with his remark, swing one back at him: "And you, are you about done chasing those girls in the mailroom? You really are a pig."
4. This will annoy your colleague and make him feel powerless.
5. Take advantage of this and finish him off with: "By the way, speaking of noses, yours is really big."
6. Sit back at your desk and enjoy feeling powerful and victorious.

Expert Opinion

According to latest studies, 77% of men believe that women go to powder their noses when they go to the toilet. Frightening!

Testimonial

"My boss always makes little comments on everything, so of course on this day I got my chance to get a swipe back. I accused him of being a pervert. Since then he hasn't said a thing. Ah, the joys of office life…"
Sophie, 35, graphic designer, Prague

Realism:	Difficulty:

APPENDIX: The Career Booster Tool Kit

This is not the kind of self-help book that gives advice on how to dramatically change your life and then leaves you to do it alone without any tools to help.

No, this is not our style of doing things. Our guide has been conceived in a way that allows you to start applying our advice as of today – and get real benefits from it.

You will see in the following pages: how to get a salary increase with the Golden Rules. Then, to help boost your career, we have prepared a tool kit that will help you put into practice the methods suggested in the book, including:

Tool 1: TML3S checklist with you, everywhere!
Tool 2: Plan your optimum safety launch window

Get A Salary Increase With this Book's Advice!

Tom Hayatt, our expert, recently published an astonishing study relating to salaries and the use of the toilets at a workplace. This study takes into account all possible parameters: profitability, punctuality, number of cases of gastroenteritis, heritable diathesis to constipation, number of hot-dog lunches per month, passion for exotic fruit, cabbage and beans and so on. The final results are more than significant:

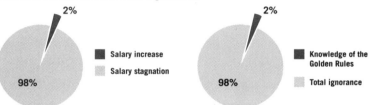

The two per cent of employees who master the Golden Rules of company toilets are the ones with the fastest salary increases.

To confirm his results, Hayatt secretly trained a group of 50 executives, known as the Golden Rules Experts, and charted their salaries:

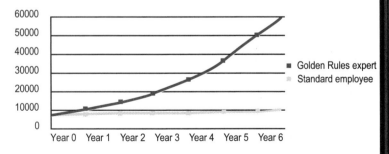

Respect the Golden Rules of this book and your salary will increase significantly in coming years!

Tool 1: TML3S checklist

Take this with you, everywhere! As you already know, TML3S is the code word of best toilet performers to defend themselves from any danger likely to happen in company toilets. It actually consists of state-of-the-art camouflage techniques, initially inspired by army special forces and created by Tom Hayatt, to safely reach company toilets.

In order for you to constantly remember TML3S, we have provided you with a special memo card to print, cut out and keep in your pocket at all times!

When you have reached the toilet, tick the boxes and check you were not caught on the way.

NB: For the most adventurous employees, we recommend laminating the card.

Tool 2: Optimum Safety Launch Window

Have you ever noticed that your colleagues and your boss usually go and do their business at the same time every day? Based on aeronautical science, we prepared a Safety Launch Window planning tool. Note when your colleagues go to the toilet. With a little work, you will get to know your Optimum Safety Launch Window.

To prevent any incidents, never name your colleagues by their real name and store this page in a safe and inaccessible zone.

Colleague no	Nickname	06:00	07:00	08:00	09:00	10:00	11:00	12:00
Example	Stinky geeky			■				
1								
2								
3								
4								
5								
6								
7								
8								
9								
10								
BOSS								
My safety launch window								

Colleague no	Nickname	13:00	14:00	15:00	16:00	17:00	18:00	19:00	20:00
Example	Stinky geeky	■							
1									
2									
3									
4									
5									
6									
7									
8									
9									
10									
BOSS									
My safety launch window									

Conclusion

Were you afraid to get caught? You now know how use the toilet without fear. Were you afraid to be judged by your behaviour? Now you know your actions are safe. Were you scared of leaving? You now know how to exit proudly.

Reading these pages, you must have marvelled at the power, realism and efficiency of our methods. We told you these methods save careers, perhaps even lives! Now you know all the potential risks, and – more importantly – the solutions to all the risky situations that you could encounter while in the toilet. Reading this book is a high-gain investment; you have a huge advantage over your colleagues. We would not be surprised if, in a few years, a serious study will show that the readers of this book have climbed the company ladder quicker than others in the hierarchy battle within your organization.

Another gain is that you can now identify others' poor behaviour: all those fools who act naively, ignorant of the Golden Rules, and their impending downfall.

You can now consider yourself as having superior knowledge compared to your boss: you will not enter the toilet at the same time as him and he will try to talk to you in the toilet. You will also be equipped with knowledge above and beyond that of your colleague who only knows how to deal with a broken toilet seat...

You are therefore solidly equipped for the corporate world, where competition rages. We have taught you how to face aggression, impose your superiority, or use your sense of humour. As this know-how makes you fittter for the professional world, make good use of it. Never use it to deliberately harm another person.

You can tell yourself that you are now one of those people who will advance faster than others. We expect the formation of an elite association that will bring together superior beings from all over the world – including you.

Yes, this book has changed your existence. You no longer see toilets as places of danger. They are territory where you can play the company's mindgames. You are no longer ignorant of toilet suvival technique, but now one of its masters!